ENGLISCH FÜR KINDER

I SPEAK ENGLISH TOO! 1

Copyright © 2022 Zigzag English / Lydia Winter

All rights reserved. No part of this publication may be reproduced or transmitted in any form without the written permission of the author.

ISBN: 978-1-914911-21-7

www.zigzagenglish.co.uk

www.zigzagenglish.co.uk – BOOKS FOR ENGLISH LEARNERS

OUR BOOKS FOR CHILDREN

Our bilingual picture books for younger children. *Funny stories in simple, useful everyday English, with colour photos.*
English with Tony -1- Tony moves house
English with Tony -2- Tony is happy
English with Tony -3- Tony's Christmas
English with Tony -4- Tony's holiday
My best friend

Our coursebook for beginners *(age 7 to 11)*
English for Children - 1st Coursebook *(Essential vocabulary and grammar for beginners)*

Our dialogue books for beginners *(age 7 to 11).*
I Speak English Too! - 1
I Speak English Too! - 2

Our series of reading and comprehension books for beginners *(age 7 to 11).*
Read English with Zigzag - 1
Read English with Zigzag - 2
Read English with Zigzag - 3
   Audiobook at Audible.com

Our vocabulary book with photos, word puzzles and more *(age 7+)*
300+ mots en anglais / 300+ englische Wörter / 300+ palabras en inglés / 300+ parole inglesi

The Learn English Activity Book for Children *(A1 - A2, elementary).*
(Recommended for children in early secondary school.)

Our series of reading and comprehension books for children at elementary level *(A1 - A2) (recommended for ages 10 to 13). With lots of language activities.*
Read English with Ben - 1
Read English with Ben - 2
Read English with Ben - 3

Our YOU DECIDE adventure book with 1 beginning and 19 endings. *A2 (11+)   Your Bilingual Fairy Tale Adventure*

Our series of reading and discussion books about a family with superpowers *(with writing tasks) for children at secondary school, A2 - B1*
I Live in a Castle – Book 1 – My Superpower
I Live in a Castle – Book 2 – The New Me

The Speak English, Read English, Write English Activity Books – 3 books from A1 to B2, for older children and adults.

Our non-fiction book with language activities
Learn English with Fun Facts! – A2 - B2

English Dialogues for Teenagers – for ages 11 to 17, A2 - B2

OUR BOOKS FOR ADULTS

Our 3 Grammar books with grammar-focused dialogues
Learn English Grammar through Conversation – A1, A2 and B1

Our Dialogue books for adults *(with vocabulary lists and comprehension questions). Audiobooks are available for some of these books – at Audible.com.*
50 very Easy Everyday English Dialogues (A2)
50 Easy Everyday English Dialogues (A2 - B1)
50 Intermediate Everyday English Dialogues (B1 - B2)
50 more Intermediate Everyday English Dialogues (B1 - B2)
40 Advanced Everyday English Dialogues (B2 - C1)
40 Intermediate Business English Dialogues (B1 - B2)
40 Advanced Business English Dialogues (B2 - C1)

Our activity books for adults and older children
The Speak English, Read English, Write English Activity Books – 3 books, for A1 - A2, A2 - B1 and B1 - B2.

Our non-fiction book with language activities
Learn English with Fun Facts! – A2 - B2

Contents

Die Ziele dieses Buches sind: 5
Unsere Methode, um Kindern im Grundschulalter Englisch beizubringen: 5
Wie man dieses Buch vewendet: 5

1A: Hello! Where do you live? 7

2A: My mum's English and my dad's German 12

3A: I like it 15

4A: Friends 20

5A: Sara's house 24

6A: Two pets 28

Word Search 1 32

7A: What time is it? 33

8A: It's cold 37

9A: What's your school like? 41

10A: Clothes 46

11A: Buying presents 50

12A: Christmas 55

Word Search 2 57

Antworten 58
Vielen Dank, dass Sie dieses Buch gelesen haben. 60
From: I Speak English Too! - 2 61
From: Read English with Zigzag – 1 62
From: The Learn English Activity Book for children 63

Die Ziele dieses Buches sind:
1. Ihrem Kind das Selbstvertrauen zu geben, Englisch zu lesen und zu sprechen.
2. Ihrem Kind Schlüsselwörter und -sätze beizubringen, die ihm dann helfen, seine Englischkenntnisse zu erweitern.

Unsere Methode, um Kindern im Grundschulalter Englisch beizubringen:
1. Diese Dialoge wurden von einer qualifizierten und erfahrenen Englischlehrerin geschrieben und mit Kindern im Alter zwischen 7 und 12 Jahren getestet.
2. Der schnellste Weg, eine Sprache zu lernen, ist durch individuelle Unterstützung. Wenn Sie ein wenig Englisch sprechen, können Sie dieses Buch benutzen, um Ihrem Kind zu helfen. Sie müssen keine Angst haben, Fehler zu machen - Sie können einfach die Sätze im Buch lesen. Wenn Sie möchten, können Sie aber auch die Dialoge verwenden, um neue Gespräche mit Ihrem Kind zu führen.
3. Die Dialoge sind natürlich auch für Geschwisterpaare geeignet.
4. Das Buch beginnt mit den Grundlagen und fügt dann Wörter und Redewendungen hinzu, um die Englischkenntnisse Ihres Kindes zu erweitern. Das Kind hat die Möglichkeit, mit "fill the gaps" und Verständnisfragen mehr aus den Dialogen zu lernen. Der Wortschatz wird auch in Wortsuchen getestet.
5. In 23 Dialogen wird Ihr Kind von "Hello. What's your name?" zu "Can you buy Christmas presents there? I want to buy presents for my family" gehen.
6. Und dann ist es bereit, mit Buch 2 fortzufahren!

Wie man dieses Buch vewendet:
1. Lesen Sie mit Ihrem Kind den Dialog A.
2. Schauen Sie sich gemeinsam die Vokabelliste an und helfen Sie Ihrem Kind bei den neuen Wörtern.
3. Tauschen Sie die Rollen und lesen Sie den Dialog erneut.
4. Ermutigen Sie Ihr Kind, die Übung zu machen. Die Übung "Fill the Gaps" (Lücken ausfüllen) kann ohne Bezugnahme auf die Originalsätze durchgeführt werden - dies ist eine lustige

Herausforderung, die es dem Kind erlaubt, alle Wörter zu verwenden, die innerhalb des Dialogs Sinn ergeben. Sie können Ihr Kind auch auffordern, die fehlenden Sätze zu suchen - diese befinden sich am Ende der Übung - und die richtigen Sätze auszuwählen. Die Antworten auf die <u>Verständnisfragen</u> befinden sich am Ende des Buches.

5. Lesen Sie den <u>Dialog B</u>. Tauschen Sie die Rollen und lesen Sie ihn erneut.

6. Stellen Sie Ihrem Kind die Fragen unter <u>C: What about you?</u>

7. Wenn Sie möchten, können Sie versuchen, mit Ihrem Kind ein Gespräch zu führen, indem Sie die Vokabeln aus den Dialogen A und B, sowie die Vokabeln aus früheren Dialogen verwenden. Sie können natürlich auch einige neue Wörter und Sätze einführen, wenn Sie möchten. Unserer Erfahrung nach ist dies die effektivste Art, einem Kind Englisch beizubringen. Sie werden Ihrem Kind helfen, seine Englischkenntnisse Tag für Tag zu erweitern.

8. Während sich das Englisch Ihres Kindes verbessert, versuchen Sie, ihm leichte englische Lese- und Hörbücher zu geben und leichte Kindersendungen im Fernsehen zu zeigen. Versuchen Sie es doch einmal mit unserer Reihe fortschreitender englischer Lesebücher für das Anfängerniveau: **Read English with Zigzag**. Es geht um eine Katze, einen Hund, einen Bruder und eine Schwester. Es ist lustig - und hat viele Bilder! Außerdem enthält es Vokabellisten, Verständnisfragen und Sprachübungen. Dazu gibt es auch ein **Hörbuch**.

9. Gehen Sie zu **Buch 2** über, um Ihrem Kind zu helfen, die nächste Stufe zu erreichen.

11. Es ist wunderbar zu sehen, wie ein Kind Fortschritte macht, vom Nichtverstehen bis hin zur Fähigkeit, ein richtiges Gespräch zu führen. Viel Glück und viel Spaß!

LESSON 1

1A: Hello! Where do you live?

Anna: Hello.

Katie: Hello. What's your name?

Anna: My name's Anna. What's your name?

Katie: I'm Katie. How are you?

Anna: I'm fine. How are you?

Katie: I'm okay, thank you. How old are you?

Anna: I'm ten. How old are you?

Katie: I'm nine. You're big! I'm small. My sister is big.

Anna: What's your sister's name and how old is she?

Katie: Her name is Jessica. She's eleven.

Anna: Where do you live?

Katie: I live in **the UK**. I live in **Cambridge**. Where do you live?

Anna: I live in Berlin, in Germany. Berlin is big. Is Cambridge small?

Katie: It's not **very** small, but it's not very big. Do you like Berlin?

Anna: Yes, I do. I like it. It's **nice**. Goodbye, Katie.

Katie: Bye, Anna.

Vocabulary
- the UK   das Vereinigte Königreich
- Cambridge – a city in the south east of England eine Stadt im Südosten Englands
- very   sehr
- nice   nett, schön

1A: Fill the gaps

Anna: Hello.

Katie:

Anna: My name's Anna. What's your name?

Katie:

Anna: I'm fine. How are you?

Katie:

Anna: I'm ten. How old are you?

Katie:

Anna: What's your sister's name and how old is she?

Katie:

Anna: Where do you live?

Katie:

Anna: I live in Berlin, in Germany. Berlin is big. Is Cambridge small?

Katie:

Anna: Yes, I do. I like it. It's nice. Goodbye, Katie.

Katie:

1. I live in the UK. I live in Cambridge. Where do you live?
2. Bye, Anna.
3. I'm Katie. How are you?
4. It's not very small, but it's not very big. Do you like Berlin?
5. Her name is Jessica. She's eleven.
6. I'm okay, thank you. How old are you?
7. Hello. What's your name?
8. I'm nine. You're big! I'm small. My sister is big.

1B

Sam: Hello!

Jack: Hello. I'm Jack. What's your name?

Sam: My name's Sam and my **big brother's** name is Andrew.

Jack: Are you okay?

Sam: Yes, I'm fine. How are you?

Jack: I'm okay, thanks.

Sam: Are you eleven?

Jack: No, I'm **not**. I'm not eleven, I'm ten. How old are you? You're big!

Sam: I'm eleven. I live in Cambridge. Do you live in Cambridge too?

Jack: Yes, I do. I live in Cambridge too. Cambridge is small.

Sam: Yes, it's **quite** small.

Jack: Bye, Sam.

Sam: Goodbye, Jack!

Vocabulary
- big brother   großer Bruder
- not   nicht
- quite   ziemlich

1C: What about you?

1. *What's your name?*
2. *How are you?*
3. *Where do you live?*

LESSON 2

2A: My mum's English and my dad's German

Anna: Hello Katie. How are you **today**?

Katie: Hi Anna. I'm fine, thanks. Is that your mum?

Anna: Yes, it is.

Katie: What's your mum's name?

Anna: Her name's Claire.

Katie: Is she nice?

Anna: Yes, she's very nice.

Katie: Is your mum German?

Anna: No, she's not. My dad's German, but my mum's not. She's English.

Katie: Does your dad **speak** English?

Anna: No, he doesn't. My mum speaks English and German. My dad speaks German, but he doesn't speak English.

Katie: My mum and dad are English. They speak English. I speak English and **a little bit** of German.

Anna: Do you really speak German? That's great!

Vocabulary
- today   heute
- to speak   sprechen
- a little bit   ein kleines bisschen

2A: Find the right answer

1. Is Anna's mum German?
    a. No, she's not, she's English.
    b. Yes, she is. She's German.
    c. No, she's not, she's American.

2. Does Anna's mum speak German?
    a. No, she doesn't, she speaks English.
    b. Yes, she does, she speaks German and English.
    c. She speaks a little bit of German.

2B

Jack: Hi, Sam.

Sam: Hi!

Jack: Are you okay?

Sam: Yes, I'm fine, thanks.

Jack: Is that boy your brother?

Sam: Yes, he's my big brother. His name's Andrew.

Jack: How old is he?

Sam: He's quite big. He's twelve.

Jack: Do you like him?

Sam: Yes, I do. I quite like him. He's okay. Do you have a brother?

Jack: No, I don't. But I have a little sister. She's very small. She's five.

Sam: Do you like her?

Jack: No, I don't. I don't like her. She's too small. She's **boring**.

Vocabulary
- boring   langweilig

2C What about you?

1. What's your mum's name?
2. Is your dad English?
3. Does your mum speak English?

LESSON 3

3A: I like it

Katie: What do you like, Anna? Do you like ice cream?

Anna: Yes, I do. I like ice cream **a lot**.

Katie: I like ice cream too. I like ice cream and **chocolate**.

Anna: I like ice cream, I like chocolate, and I like chocolate ice cream!

Katie: What don't you like?

Anna: I don't like **peas**. I **really** don't like them!

Katie: Do you like your house?

Anna: Yes, I do. My house is very nice. It's quite big.

Katie: I like my bedroom. It's quite small, but I like it.

Anna: What colour is your bedroom?

Katie: It's green.

Anna: Green is a nice colour. Is it your **favourite** colour?

Katie: No, it's not. I like green, but my favourite colour is red.

Anna: I like green and red too. My favourite colour is orange. My bedroom is blue, but my **bed** is orange. I love it!

Vocabulary
- a lot   sehr
- chocolate   Schokolade
- pea   Erbse
- really   wirklich
- favourite colour   Lieblingsfarbe
- bed   Bett

3A: Fill the gaps

Katie: What do you like, Anna? Do you like ice cream?

Anna:

Katie: I like ice cream too. I like ice cream and chocolate.

Anna: I like ice cream, I like chocolate, and I like chocolate ice cream!

Katie: What don't you like?

Anna:

Katie:

Anna: Yes, I do. My house is very nice. It's quite big.

Katie: I like my bedroom. It's quite small, but I like it.

Anna:

Katie: It's green.

Anna: Green is a nice colour. Is it your favourite colour?

Katie:

Anna: I like green and red too. My favourite colour is orange. My bedroom is blue, but my bed is orange. I love it!

1. Do you like your house?
2. No, it's not. I like green, but my favourite colour is red.
3. What colour is your bedroom?
4. I don't like peas. I really don't like them!
5. Yes, I do. I like ice cream a lot.

 3B

Sam: Do you have a dog, Jack?

Jack: No, I don't. **But** I have a very nice cat.

Sam: What colour is your cat? Is it black and white?

Jack: No, it's not. It's brown and white. Do you have a cat **too**?

Sam: No, I don't have a cat. My dad doesn't like cats. But I have a dog.

Jack: Do you have a big dog or a small dog?

Sam: It's not very big. It's quite small.

Jack: What colour is it?

Sam: It's black.

Jack: What's its name?

Sam: Its name is Fluffy.

Jack: Fluffy is a nice name. I like dogs. I **want** a dog.

Sam: You want a dog and I want a cat!

Vocabulary
- but   aber
- too   auch
- to want   wollen

3C What about you?

1. *What do you like?*
2. *What don't you like?*
3. *Do you have a cat?*
4. *Do you want a dog?*

LESSON 4

4A: Friends

Katie: **How many** friends do you have, Anna?

Anna: I have quite a lot of friends. I have six or seven friends. Do you have a lot of friends?

Katie: No, I don't. I have three friends.

Anna: Do you have a **best friend**?

Katie: Yes, I do. My best friend's name is Ben.

Anna: I have a best friend too. Her name's Sara. She's ten.

Katie: What does she **look like**?

Anna: She's very **tall**. She's quite **thin**.

Katie: Ben is **short**. He's a bit **fat**. He's a very nice boy. I like him a lot.

Anna: How many brothers and **sisters** does he have?

Katie: He has two brothers and two sisters. He has a big **family**.

Anna: Sara has a small family. She has no brothers or sisters. But she has a lot of friends.

Katie: Does she speak English?

Anna: She speaks a little bit of English. And a lot of German!

Vocabulary
- how many   wie viele
- best friend   bester Freund
- to look like   aussehen wie
- tall   groß
- thin   dünn
- short   klein
- fat   dick
- sister   Schwester
- family   Familie

4A: Find the right answer

1. What is Anna's best friend's name?
    a. It's Ben
    b. Her best friend's name is Sara.
    c. She doesn't have a best friend.

2. Does Sara speak English?
    a. Yes, she speaks a lot of English.
    b. No, she doesn't speak English.
    c. Yes, she speaks a little bit of English.

3. How many friends does Anna have?
    a. She has three friends.
    b. She doesn't have a lot of friends.
    c. She has quite a lot of friends.

4. How many brothers and sisters does Ben have?
    a. He has a big family. He has three brothers and two sisters.
    b. He has no brothers or sisters. His family's small.
    c. He has four brothers and sisters.

5. Is Sara short and thin?
    a. Yes, she is. She's short and thin.
    b. No, she's not. She's short and fat.
    c. She's thin, but she's not short.

4B

Sam: Do you like my big brother, Jack?

Jack: Your brother Andrew? Yes, I do. He's nice. I like him. He's very tall, isn't he?

Sam: Yes, he's quite tall. What does your little sister look like?

Jack: She's not tall. She's very short. She's quite fat. She has **long** brown hair. She has big brown eyes.

Sam: Andrew has short **fair** hair and blue eyes.

Jack: You have short fair hair too. But you don't have blue eyes. You have brown eyes, don't you?

Sam: Yes, I do. What's your sister's favourite colour?

Jack: It's yellow. She likes yellow a lot. What's Andrew's favourite colour?

Sam: I don't know.

Vocabulary
- long   lang
- fair   blond

4C What about you?

1. How many friends do you have?
2. Do you have a best friend?
3. What does your friend look like?
4. What's your friend's favourite colour?

LESSON 5

5A: Sara's house

Katie: **Where** does your best friend live, Anna?

Anna: My friend Sara?

Katie: Yes. Does she live in Berlin?

Anna: Yes, she does. She lives **near** my house.

Katie: What's her house like? Does she live in a big house?

Anna: No, she doesn't. Her house isn't very big, because she has a small family. But it's quite nice. It has a **beautiful garden**.

Katie: How many **bedrooms** does her house have?

Anna: It has two bedrooms. Does your house have two bedrooms too?

Katie: No, there are three bedrooms in my house. One for me, one for my sister and one for my **parents**.

Anna: What's your **living room** like?

Katie: We have a **lovely** living room. It has a big blue sofa and an **enormous television**. The living room is my favourite room.

Vocabulary
- where — wo
- near — nahe
- beautiful — schön
- garden — Garten
- bedroom — Schlafzimmer
- parents — Eltern
- living room — Wohnzimmer
- lovely — schön
- enormous — riesig
- television — Fernseher

5A: Fill the gaps

Katie: Where does your best friend live, Anna?

Anna: My friend Sara?

Katie: Yes. Does she live in Berlin?

Anna:

Katie: What's her house like? Does she live in a big house?

Anna:

Katie: How many bedrooms does her house have?

Anna:

Katie: No, there are three bedrooms in my house. One for me, one for my sister and one for my parents.

Anna: What's your living room like?

Katie:

1. No, she doesn't. Her house isn't very big, because she has a small family. But it's quite nice. It has a beautiful garden.
2. We have a lovely living room. It has a big blue sofa and an enormous television. The living room is my favourite room.
3. It has two bedrooms. Does your house have two bedrooms too?
4. Yes, she does. She lives near my house.

5B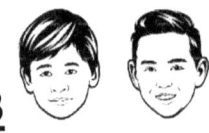

Sam: Where do you live, Jack? Is your house near here? Is it near the park?

Jack: No, it's not. It's near the big Tesco's supermarket.

Sam: I live quite near the park. Not **far** from the **cinema**.

Jack: What's your house like?

Sam: I live in a **flat**. It's very small. It has two bedrooms – one for my parents and one for me and my brother.

Jack: Does it have a nice living room?

Sam: No, not really. The living room is **tiny**.

Jack: Do you have a garden?

Sam: No, we don't. But we live near the park, so that's okay.

Vocabulary
- far   weit
- cinema   Kino
- flat   Wohnung
- tiny   winzig

5C What about you?

1. Where does your friend live?
2. What's your friend's house like?
3. How many bedrooms does your house have?
4. Does it have a nice living room?

LESSON 6

6A: Two pets

Katie: Do you like **animals**, Anna?

Anna: Yes, **of course** I do. I love animals.

Katie: Do you have a **pet**?

Anna: Yes, I have two pets. I have a **rabbit** and a **hamster**.

Katie: Why do you have a rabbit AND a hamster?

Anna: Because one pet isn't **enough**. I don't want a rabbit OR a hamster – I want **both**!

Katie: Do your parents like your two pets?

Anna: No, not really. But my friends like them.

Katie: Hamsters are okay; but I don't like rabbits.

Anna: Why not? Why don't you like them?

Katie: Because they **bite**!

Vocabulary
- animal — Tier
- of course — natürlich
- pet — Haustier
- rabbit — Kaninchen
- enough — genug
- both — beide
- to bite — beißen

6A: Find the right answer

1. Does Anna hate animals?
    a. No, she doesn't. She quite likes animals.
    b. She doesn't hate them but she doesn't like them.
    c. Of course not! She loves animals!

2. How many pets does Anna have?
    a. She has one pet. It's a cat.
    b. She has two pets – a rabbit and a hamster.
    c. She doesn't have any pets.

3. Who likes Anna's pets?
    a. Her parents like them.
    b. Her friends like them.
    c. Katie likes them.

6B

Jack: I really want a dog, Sam.

Sam: Don't you have a cat?

Jack: Yes, I do. I like my cat, but I want a dog too.

Sam: Dogs are nice, but they're very **messy**.

Jack: Cats aren't messy. But they're a bit boring.

Sam: Cats are beautiful. I want a cat, but my dad doesn't want one.

Jack: Does your mum want a cat?

Sam: Yes, she does. She likes cats a lot. But my dad really doesn't like them.

Jack: Does your brother like cats **or** dogs?

Sam: He likes **snakes**.

Jack: Snakes? I **hate** snakes!

Vocabulary
- messy   schmutzig
- or   oder
- snake   Schlange
- to hate   hassen

C What about you?

1. Do you have a pet?
2. Do you like animals?
3. Does your mum like snakes?

Word Search 1

```
W K V V G A G Y P T Y W F L V
I G M A Q F A X E T E T M J C
H T A I V O R U T I N Y Q B H
D U P Y B N D U S Q E G U O O
M G C L O V E L Y E A G I R C
P E W U S E N E F R R R T I O
R I M Z H R Y S H O R T E N L
K C H K I Y A T I P L M W G A
N H M R N K E A D A V M A W T
Q Y C Y G T A U L R R W J Y E
S W F W W L I V R E X F Z E Y
H Z D D Y B L U K N Y U B R L
F A V O U R I T E T B C P Q I
O R I V H Z B S A S Y A X Y C
V T V H O Y H N Y M H B U T W
```

- I love 🍫, but I don't like ice cream.
- Your mum and dad are tall, but my **p_re_t_** are **s_or_**.
- I don't like your house. It's too small – it's **t_ny**! But your **g_rd_n** is **l_ve_y**!
- My best friend has a **_er_** nice **p_t**. It's a cat.
- What's your **fa_our_te** pet? Dogs. Hamsters are **q_it_** nice too, but rabbits are **b_r_ng**.
- Do you live **n_ar** the cinema?

LESSON 7

7A: What time is it?

Katie: What time is it in Berlin, Anna?

Anna: It's two o'clock.

Katie: Two o'clock? It's one o'clock here. It's **early**.

Anna: Do you have school today?

Katie: No, I don't. Are you at school?

Anna: Yes, I am.

Katie: What time do you **go to school**?

Anna: I **get up** at half past six. I go to school at half past seven. I **start** school at eight o'clock.

Katie: I start school at a quarter to nine. I get up at eight o'clock, and **run** to school! Do you **walk** to school?

Anna: Yes, I walk to school. It's near my house.

Vocabulary
- early   früh
- to go to school   zur Schule gehen

- to get up   aufstehen
- to start   beginnen
- to run   laufen
- to walk   zu Fuß gehen

7A: Fill the gaps

Katie: What time is it in Berlin, Anna?

Anna:

Katie: Two o'clock? It's one o'clock here. It's early.

Anna:

Katie: No, I don't. Are you at school?

Anna:

Katie: What time do you go to school?

Anna:

Katie: I start school at a quarter to nine. I get up at eight o'clock, and run to school! Do you walk to school?

Anna:
1. Yes, I am.
2. Do you have school today?
3. Yes, I walk to school. It's near my house.
4. I get up at half past six. I go to school at half past seven. I start school at eight o'clock.
5. It's two o'clock.

7B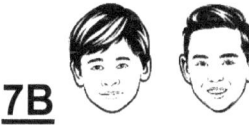

Sam: Do you like school, Jack?

Jack: No, not really. School starts too early. It starts at ten to nine.

Sam: That *is* early. My school starts at a quarter past nine.

Jack: What time is your **lunch break**?

Sam: We have lunch at twenty to one.

Jack: And **when** do you go **home**?

Sam: At a quarter to four.

Jack: That's quite **late**. We go home at five past three.

Sam: When do you **do your homework**?

Jack: I don't have a lot of homework. My mum **drives** me to school, and I do my homework in the **car**!

Vocabulary
- lunch break   Mittagspause
- when   wann
- home   [nach] Hause
- late   spät
- to do homework   Hausaufgaben machen
- to drive   fahren
- car   Auto

7C What about you?

1. What time is it?
2. What time do you go to school?
3. What time do you have lunch?
4. Do you walk or run to school?
5. Do you have a lot of homework?

LESSON 8

8A: It's cold

Anna: Is it cold in Cambridge? It's not cold in Berlin. It's quite warm.

Katie: It's cold here. My house is quite cold. But my school is too **hot**.

Anna: Where are you? Are you at school?

Katie: No. I'm in my bedroom.

Anna: I'm in my bedroom too.

Katie: Is your sister **there**?

Anna: No, she's in the **kitchen**. But my friend Sara is **here**.

Katie: Where are your pets?

Anna: My rabbit's here, in my bedroom. But my hamster is in my sister's bedroom.

Katie: Does your sister like your hamster?

Anna: Yes, she loves my hamster. She wants my hamster to live in her bedroom. But she doesn't really like my rabbit.

Katie: Why not? Does your rabbit bite?

Anna: **Maybe** a little bit.

Vocabulary
- cold — kalt
- hot — heiß
- there — dort
- kitchen — Küche
- here — hier
- maybe — vielleicht

8A: Find the answers

1. Is it cold in Berlin?
    a. Yes, it is. It's quite cold.
    b. No, it's not. It's quite warm.
    c. Yes, it is. It's cold and rainy.

2. Where's Sara?
    a. She's at home.
    b. She's in Cambridge.
    c. She's in Anna's bedroom.

3. Why doesn't Anna's sister like her rabbit?
    a. Because it bites.
    b. Because it's boring.
    c. Because it's not a hamster.

8B

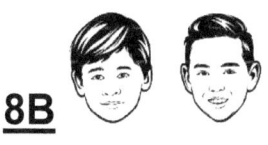

Sam: It's really cold today.

Jack: It's **always** cold in Cambridge.

Sam: No, it's not; not always.

Jack: When it's not cold, it **rains**.

Sam: No; **sometimes** it's hot and **sunny**.

Jack: I'm cold. I'm very cold.

Sam: Do you want to go home?

Jack: Yes, I do. Do you want to **come** to my house?

Sam: Is your house cold too?

Jack: No, it's not. It's really warm in my house.

Sam: Great! **Let's go**!

Vocabulary
- always — immer
- to rain — regnen
- sometimes — manchmal
- sunny — sonnig
- to come — kommen
- let's go — gehen wir / lass uns gehen

8C What about you?

1. Is it cold today? Or is it hot and sunny?
2. Where are you?

LESSON 9

9A: What's your school like?

Anna: What's your school like, Katie? Is it nice?

Katie: It's okay. I quite like it. Do you like your school?

Anna: Yes, I do. It's a very good school.

Katie: How big is the school?

Anna: It's big. There are **about** five **hundred children**.

Katie: **How many** boys and how many girls are there?

Anna: I don't know. But there are fifteen girls and ten boys in my class.

Katie: That's a lot of girls.

Anna: Yes. Do you have a lot of girls in your class?

Katie: No. **Half** my class are boys.

Anna: Is your best friend in your class?

Katie: No. He doesn't go to my school. He goes to a **different** school.

Anna: Oh, that's bad **luck**.

Vocabulary
- about   ungefähr, etwa
- hundred   hundert
- children   Kinder
- how many   wie viele
- half   die Hälfte
- different   anderer
- luck   Glück

9A: Fill the gaps

Anna:

Katie: It's okay. I quite like it. Do you like your school?

Anna:

Katie: How big is the school?

Anna:

Katie: How many boys and how many girls are there?

Anna:

Katie: That's a lot of girls.

Anna:

Katie: No. Half my class are boys.

Anna:

Katie: No. He doesn't go to my school. He goes to a different school.

Anna:

1. I don't know. But there are fifteen girls and ten boys in my class.
2. Oh, that's bad luck.
3. Yes, I do. It's a very good school.
4. Is your best friend in your class?
5. It's big. There are about five hundred children.
6. Yes. Do you have a lot of girls in your class?
7. What's your school like, Katie? Is it nice?

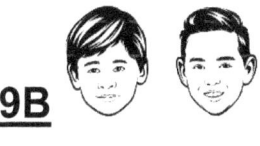

9B

Sam: What are the **teachers** like at your school?

Jack: They're not bad. We have **some** very good teachers.

Sam: **What's your teacher called?**

Jack: She's called Mrs Brown. Her **husband works** at the school too.

Sam: What does he do? Is he a teacher too?

Jack: No. He's a **cook**. He cooks our school **lunches**.

Sam: Is he a good cook?

Jack: I **think** so. We have a lot of fish and chips. I love fish and chips!

Sam: I don't have school lunches. I **take** sandwiches to school.

Jack: Don't you think sandwiches are boring?

Sam: Yes, they are a bit boring. I have **cheese** sandwiches **every day**!

Vocabulary
- teacher — Lehrer
- some — einige
- what's…called? — wie heißt…
- husband — Mann
- to work — arbeiten
- cook — Koch
- lunch — Mittagessen
- to think — Ich denke schon
- to take — mitnehmen
- cheese — Käse
- every day — jeden Tag

9C What about you?

1. How big is your school?
2. How many children are there in your class?
3. What's your teacher called?
4. Do you take sandwiches to school?

LESSON 10

10A: Clothes

Anna: Does your school have a uniform, Katie?

Katie: Yes, of course it does. Don't all schools have a school uniform?

Anna: No. My school doesn't. Lots of schools in Germany don't.

Katie: Really? **Lucky** you! I hate my school uniform.

Anna: **Why** do you hate it? What is your uniform?

Katie: Girls and boys all wear black **trousers**, a white **shirt** and a purple top.

Anna: That sounds okay. What's wrong with that?

Katie: Some girls don't like trousers. They want to wear **skirts**.

Anna: So do the boys like the uniform?

Katie: No, not really. Lots of boys don't like purple.

Anna: Why not? I love purple. I **often** wear purple tops to school.

Katie: **Seriously**?!

Vocabulary
- lucky you!   Glück gehabt!
- why   warum
- trousers   Hose
- shirt   Hemd
- skirt   Rock
- often   oft
- seriously?   ernsthaft?

10B

Sam: Do you like **shopping**, Jack?

Jack: Yes, I love shopping. I like **buying** new **clothes** with my mum.

Sam: **How often** do you buy new clothes?

Jack: Quite often. Maybe **once a month**.

Sam: I like new clothes too. But my mum says they're too **expensive**.

Jack: Some clothes shops are **cheap**. And buying online is cheap too.

Sam: I really want some new **trainers**. But the ones I like are very expensive.

Jack: Maybe **wait** till **Christmas**?

Sam: What do you want for Christmas?

Jack: I want a new **jacke**t. A beautiful red one. It's online.

Sam: Is it cheap?

Jack: No, not really. But it's for Christmas!

Vocabulary
- to shop — einkaufen
- to buy — kaufen
- new — neu
- clothes — Kleidung
- how often — wie oft
- once a month — einmal im Monat
- expensive — teuer
- cheap — billig
- trainers — Turnschuhe
- to wait — warten
- till — bis
- Christmas — Weihnachten
- jacket — Jacke

10A / 10b: Answer the questions

1. What is Katie's school uniform?

2. How often does Jack go shopping?
3. Does Jack want some new trainers for Christmas?

10C: What about you?

1. Does your school have a uniform?
2. Do you like shopping?
3. What do you want for Christmas?

LESSON 11

11A: Buying presents

Anna: It's almost Christmas!

Katie: Yes, it is. I want to buy my sister a **present**. But I don't know what to get her.

Anna: What does she want?

Katie: I don't know.

Anna: What does she like?

Katie: She likes clothes, music and animals.

Anna: Does she like dogs?

Katie: Yes, she loves them.

Anna: Why don't you get her a dog?

Katie: A dog? I really don't think my parents want a dog.

Anna: Okay. Maybe buy her a **dress** or a jacket.

Katie: They're too expensive. I don't have a lot of **money**.

Anna: Is it cold in Cambridge?

Katie: Yes, it's very cold.

Anna: What about a **hat**?

Katie: Good **idea**! Thanks!

Vocabulary
- present   Geschenk
- dress   Kleid
- money   Geld
- hat   Hut
- idea   Idee

11A: Fill the gaps

Anna:

Katie: Yes, it is. I want to buy my sister a present. But I don't know what to get her.

Anna:

Katie: I don't know.

Anna:

Katie: She likes clothes, music and animals.

Anna:

Katie: Yes, she loves them.

Anna:

Katie: A dog? I really don't think my parents want a dog.

Anna:

Katie: They're too expensive. I don't have a lot of money.

Anna:

Katie: Yes, it's very cold.

Anna:

Katie: Good idea! Thanks!

    1. Is it cold in Cambridge?
    2. What about a hat?
    3. Does she like dogs?
    4. What does she like?
    5. It's almost Christmas!

6. Okay. Maybe buy her a dress or a jacket.
7. What does she want?
8. Why don't you get her a dog?

11B

Sam: Do you want to go to the Christmas **market**, Jack?

Jack: **Where** is it?

Sam: It's in the **city centre**.

Jack: Is it good?

Sam: Yes, it's great. There are nice **things** to **eat** and **drink**.

Jack: Can you buy Christmas presents there? I want to buy presents for my family.

Sam: Yes, there are lots of things to buy.

Jack: Is it expensive?

Sam: I think it's quite expensive. But if you like, we can go to the **shops** too.

Jack: Yes, that **sounds good**. When do you want to go?

Sam: How about Saturday **afternoon**?

Jack: Yes, Saturday's good. See you **then**.

Vocabulary
- market — Markt
- where — wo
- city centre — Stadtzentrum
- thing — Sache
- to eat — essen
- to drink — trinken
- shop — Geschäft
- sounds good — klingt gut
- afternoon — Nachmittag
- then — dann

11C: What about you?

1. What does your mum want for Christmas?
2. Is it cheap or expensive?

LESSON 12

12A: Christmas

Katie: What's Christmas like in Germany?

Anna: It's great. We get presents. We see all our family and eat lots of food!

Katie: We eat lots of food too, and Father Christmas brings us presents on **Christmas Day**.

Anna: Do you go to **church** at Christmas?

Katie: My family doesn't.

Anna: My school has a Christmas party. I love it!

Katie: At schools in the UK, there's **always** a Christmas **play**. All the little children are in the play.

Anna: I hope you have a good Christmas, Katie.

Katie: You too, Anna. **Merry Christmas**!

Vocabulary
- Christmas Day — Weihnachtstag
- church — Kirche
- always — immer
- play — Theaterstück

- Merry Christmas!   Frohe Weihnachten!

12B: What about you?

1. *What do you have to eat at Christmas?*
2. *Do you go to church at Christmas?*
3. *Does Father Christmas bring you presents?*

Word Search 2

```
Z D J H E P G R D L U N C H Z
I M Z K C D Z R J T Z J H N H
X C M P L B R C W Y P J E O I
J H O K T R A I N E R S A R N
V T E Q R L U C K Y F U P Q O
Y V A B O U T Z C Q Q N B K B
C R C H U R C H G C H N F Q A
V T P R S H B A L W A Y S E O
R A M D E A R L Y Y W J U N S
G W V Z R T M F Y H F X E P F
P D D V S M B W Q U V O Y P P
G D F H L O P Z U F V Z D S A
V H K C U W A U B W T Q B L B
H A D W S D Z P S A Q Q J Y Z
N Y E Q Y N D W U H O M E S G
```

- My school doesn't have a uniform. I wear **tr_in_rs** and **tr_us_rs** to school.
- Do you **a_w_ys** have **l_n_h** at school, or do you sometimes eat it at **h_m_**?
- You're **l_c_y**! You start school late. But I start school **_ar_y**.
- On Sunday, we go to 🏠 at **ab_ut h_lf** past ten.
- It sometimes rains in the summer. But it's often **s_n_y**.
- I want to buy a **_hea_** present for my friend, because I don't have a lot of money.

Antworten

Dialogue 2A: Find the right answer

1: a
2: b

Dialogue 4A: Find the right answer

1: b
2: c
3: c
4: c

Dialogue 6A: Find the right answer

1: c
2: b
3: b

Dialogue 8A Find the right answer

1: b
2: c
3: a

Dialogues 10A / 10B: Answer the questions

1. It's black trousers, a white shirt and a purple top.
2. He goes shopping about once a month.
3. No, he wants a new red jacket for Christmas.

W	K	V	V	G	A	G	Y	P	T	Y	W	F	L	V
I	G	M	A	Q	F	A	X	E	T	E	T	M	J	C
H	T	A	I	V	O	R	U	T	I	N	Y	Q	B	H
D	U	P	Y	B	N	D	U	S	Q	E	G	U	O	O
M	G	C	L	O	V	E	L	Y	E	A	G	I	R	C
P	E	W	U	S	E	N	E	F	R	R	R	T	I	O
R	I	M	Z	H	R	Y	S	H	O	R	T	E	N	L
K	C	H	K	I	Y	A	T	I	P	L	M	W	G	A
N	H	M	R	N	K	E	A	D	A	V	M	A	W	T
Q	Y	C	Y	G	T	A	U	L	R	R	W	J	Y	E
S	W	F	W	W	L	I	V	R	E	X	F	Z	E	Y
H	Z	D	D	Y	B	L	U	K	N	Y	U	B	R	L
F	A	V	O	U	R	I	T	E	T	B	C	P	Q	I
O	R	I	V	H	Z	B	S	A	S	Y	A	X	Y	C
V	T	V	H	O	Y	H	N	Y	M	H	B	U	T	W

Z	D	J	H	E	P	G	R	D	L	U	N	C	H	Z
I	M	Z	K	C	D	Z	R	J	T	Z	J	H	N	H
X	C	M	P	L	B	R	C	W	Y	P	J	E	O	I
J	H	O	K	T	R	A	I	N	E	R	S	A	R	N
V	T	E	Q	R	L	U	C	K	Y	F	U	P	Q	O
Y	V	A	B	O	U	T	Z	C	Q	Q	N	B	K	B
C	R	C	H	U	R	C	H	G	C	H	N	F	Q	A
V	T	P	R	S	H	B	A	L	W	A	Y	S	E	O
R	A	M	D	E	A	R	L	Y	Y	W	J	U	N	S
G	W	V	Z	R	T	M	F	Y	H	F	X	E	P	F
P	D	D	V	S	M	B	W	Q	U	V	O	Y	P	P
G	D	F	H	L	O	P	Z	U	F	V	Z	D	S	A
V	H	K	C	U	W	A	U	B	W	T	Q	B	L	B
H	A	D	W	S	D	Z	P	S	A	Q	Q	J	Y	Z
N	Y	E	Q	Y	N	D	W	U	H	O	M	E	S	G

Vielen Dank, dass Sie dieses Buch gelesen haben.

Wenn Sie Fragen oder Vorschläge zur Verbesserung des Buches haben, schicken Sie mir bitte eine E-Mail an: lydiawinter.zigzagenglish@gmail.com. Vorschläge für neue Bücher sind auch immer willkommen.

Die Website finden Sie hier: **www.zigzagenglish.co.uk**. Auf dieser Website können Sie und Ihr Kind sich über unsere anderen Bücher für Kinder und Erwachsene informieren und unseren Blog lesen. Sie finden dort auch weitere englischsprachige Aktivitäten.

Ich würde mich freuen, wenn Sie eine Buchrezension hinterlassen. Vielen Dank!

Hier sind einige Auszüge aus unseren anderen Büchern für Kinder, die anfangen, Englisch zu lernen:

From: I Speak English Too! - 2

8A: A week's holiday

Katie: It's my **half term** holiday next week. A **whole** week with no school!

Anna: Are you going **away**?

Katie: Yes. We're going to the Lake District.

Anna: What's that? Where is it?

Katie: It's in the **north** of England. There are lots of **mountains** and **lakes**. It's very beautiful.

Anna: Lucky you! I have school next week.

Katie: School is really hard at the moment. I'm tired. I need a **break**.

Anna: Is your whole family going?

Katie: No. My mum has to work next week. So she's **staying** at home.

Anna: Your **poor** mum.

From: Read English with Zigzag – 1

16. Too many boys and girls

Hi there! Is it your birthday today?

It's Poppy's birthday today. Poppy is nine today.

I don't like birthday parties. They're **noisy**. They're too noisy. There are lots of children. There are too many children.

Pam likes birthday parties. She likes noisy children. She likes eating birthday cake too.

I can't sit on my sofa. There are too many children in the living room! I can't eat my cat food. There are too many children in the kitchen! I can't look for a spider in the garden. That's **right** – there are too many boys and girls there!

Mum and Dad's bedroom is **quiet**. Their bed is quite comfortable.

See you tomorrow...

From: The Learn English Activity Book for Children

CHOOSE!

You can't always have everything you want.
Sometimes you have to choose.
So what do you choose?

- Ice cream or chocolate?
- A hamster or a rabbit?
- Homework or **housework**?
- A holiday at the beach or a skiing holiday?
- One very good friend or three good friends?
- Football or swimming?
- A green bedroom or a white bedroom?
- Autumn or spring?
- Chinese food or Italian food?
- Very hot **weather** or very cold weather?
- Orange juice or a milkshake?

www.ingramcontent.com/pod-product-compliance
Lightning Source LLC
LaVergne TN
LVHW021736060526
838200LV00052B/3305